LITTLE GLASS PLANET

Also by Dobby Gibson

Polar
Skirmish
It Becomes You

LITTLE GLASS PLANET

POEMS

DOBBY GIBSON

Graywolf Press

This publication is made possible, in part, by the voters of Minnesota through a Minnesota State Arts Board Operating Support grant, thanks to a legislative appropriation from the arts and cultural heritage fund. Significant support has also been provided by Target, the McKnight Foundation, the Lannan Foundation, the Amazon Literary Partnership, and other generous contributions from foundations, corporations, and individuals. To these organizations and individuals we offer our heartfelt thanks.

Published by Graywolf Press
250 Third Avenue North, Suite 600
Minneapolis, Minnesota 55401

www.graywolfpress.org

Published in the United States of America

ISBN 978-1-55597-842-6

2 4 6 8 9 7 5 3 1
First Graywolf Printing, 2019

Library of Congress Control Number: 2018958150

Cover design: Jeenee Lee Design

Cover art: Yuji Agematsu. *Zip: 01.01.14 . . . 12.31.14* (details). Mixed media in cigarette pack cellophane wrappers (365 units). On wood-backed acrylic shelves, latex paint (12 units). Wrappers, each approx.: 2½ x 2⅛ x 1 inches (6.3 x 5.3 x 2.5 cm). Courtesy of the artist, Yale Union, Portland, and Miguel Abreu Gallery, New York. Photo: Aaron Flint Jamison and Scott Ponik.

Contents

LITTLE GLASS PLANET

Dear Reader

Though we've done this many times before
it doesn't make it any less miraculous
that a fugitive intimacy can sequester itself
in the nearly invisible here
dissolving an entire alphabet into thoughts
strung from more distant thoughts like stars
inside a strange machine
that counts on you to propel it

with a joule of your mind's breath
pushing young ships into the harbor
where they ferry the very idea
that music needs no mediation
tacking this way and then that
as if each to earn the name
we moments ago christened them with
INTUITION   LAYAWAY   LAST HOPE

new fleets drifting off as older ones threaten return
across soft borders some smuggling some gone
long enough to reappear as unrecognizable
as paint swatches read differently in the sun
another among the infinite things that blue-green
never names but still colors wildly
in the spell that watches over you as you lie awake
a little longer wondering what happens to the hours

Prayer for November

Brazen angels, stubborn saboteurs
send us a sign.

Silent priests of the coat check,
cherubs of every appetite, all the powers of ten,
if we can believe in you, we can believe again.

Assure us we'll be spared. Tell us it's been you
ghostwriting our astonishing memoirs all along.

Loyal docents, restless spirits of lost chess-masters,
dogs with one eye, lead us home.
Spray-paint the orange X on our doors
and place the warm coin into our hands.

Promise it won't end in any of the ways
we think it will. Pile snow onto the capitol
and fossilize the partisans. Stuff sawdust
into the senators' crooked mouths
and announce the lies have all been told.
Spoon the cure onto every cracked tongue—
then kiss the food right down our throats.

Afternoon breeze of one syllable,
arsonists with no matches, stab wounds
healing into smiles, taxis at midnight, shine on.
Shine your penlights into the backs of our eyes
and swear you see no blindness.
Whisper the forgotten melody into our ears.
Show the skywriters how to spell
without looking back, we've been fools,
we've wasted more than we've saved,
we can be loved after all.

Elegy for Abe Vigoda

The most horrible person
has been elected president.
The hardest thing to fathom
is the present. Familiar sounds arrive
at my door from the school down the street.
The kid with the freshest haircut
holds a rubber football while hosting
a Chautauqua on defensive pass interference.
Seven students stand at the back
of the orchestra, stoned with percussion.
For the thirty-third time in her life
a science teacher announces the oldest
layer of rock is called Precambrian.
They've trained us to believe anything.
So is the rumor true? Yes, Abe Vigoda has died.
That name, like something resurrected
from a dictionary. *Abe*: another word
for honesty. And *vigoda*, meaning:
a sacred temple for vampires.
About the past I never feel the same way twice.
When I was sick and my father somewhere
across the planet, a Trinitron television
wheeled into my bedroom dispensed the medicine
of Abe Vigoda by slow drip.
I could hear the ice thunder
as it calved in the pond across the street.
Like a superhero with the powers
of an exhausted mime, Abe Vigoda cured
my fear of ghosts while teaching me
how to wear the suit of adulthood
the right amount reluctantly,
and holster my revolver behind
my back where I can never reach it.

My father is again far from me,
visiting the clinic where they treat
idiopathic positional vertigo
by reorienting the crystals of the inner ear,
which once helped him toss
exceptional spirals timed perfectly
so that as I caught or not
the football I crashed into arbor vitae
that was the closest thing I had
to a brother pummeling wisdom into me.
The past is surprisingly punctual.
All of time is with us here,
each next moment waiting right where we left it
when we last felt safe inside our heads
wondering what kind of leathery faces
they might grow into as we held
the flashlight beneath our chins
to say the one funny thing we needed to
while leaning into the dark.

Idaho

The best thing about riding a horse
is the better shadow you make. The best part
of the better shadow is knowing only half
of what it's thinking. Even doing nothing is a form
of moving on. Through the white pines
the horses walk single file, in a sentence, each rider
another noun aspiring to the verb *to be*.
The forest has no replica. Its beasts disprove everything.
At dusk, your worries are a sack of rabbits
you have to carry down to the river
and press slowly beneath the surface
until you feel it go still. In the morning,
when you wake, you'll think you stitched
the valley back together by opening your eyes.

L'Avenir Est Quelque Chose

All day for too long
everything I've thought to say
has been about umbrellas.
It's hard to remember how
I came to possess whichever one
I find in my hand, or hanging there now
upside-down in the closet like sleeping bats,
each one too tiny or huge,
like our own ideas, always needing
to be shaken off and folded up
before we can properly forget them on the train.
Most of my predictions are honestly
just hopes: a sudden sundress in March,
regime change in the North,
or the one where Amanda
wins the big book award from the baby boomers.
There's that green-and-white umbrella
the cereal-company interns handed us
outside the doomed ball game,
the one for sun,
the one with a wooden handle
as crooked as the future
we reach for whenever one of us
needs a stand-in for a dance partner.
You once opened it in the living room
so Scarlett could have a picnic
beneath what felt to her like a tent,
as it felt to me like my prediction
we would live forever was already true.
When trying to understand I tend to look up
and occasionally spot nothing
more than a thousand pinholes in black nylon,
it's enough to get you to Greece and back,

or something to kiss beneath,
who knows how this is going to play out?
I know you won't ever be able to say
exactly what you're feeling either.
The way thoughts pop open overhead
as we pull closer to what's between us,
the rain playing the drum
that's suddenly us.

Drone

Isn't this the life
Weren't the white feathers
     feathering the young

Shouldn't the invention solve the disease
Didn't the guilt end with the getaway
Aren't you the clever one

For the splash of silver sense
For the fountainry of phonemes
For a grownup desk job

And without winter
Without any equinox or ration

In the cast that hasn't dried
In the sutures of our own skin
Weren't the Lilliputians sweet

Everybody crossing their eyes sees the figure eight
Everyone's a satellite
Everyone becomes that star
Everybody dance everybody get out

Will the mouse outrun the hawk
Will the impulse to resist bring a will to surrender
Will the owner of a green Subaru Outback
     please report to the Fan Information Booth
     on Concourse C

Did we ever doubt our devices
Did we punch the right holes in the earth
Did the queen smash her bottle across
     the hull did the little ones toe the line

Was 16 the correct number
Was the whispering coming from inside the hut
Was the instant they stopped running
          the moment the verdict was returned
Was the balcony high enough for a view

Aren't you glad you're more headlight than deer
Aren't the birds quiet before they strike

Isn't the view marvelous
Isn't the hum like hearing a needle sew
Isn't the technology immaculate

Shouldn't this much be obvious
Shouldn't we praise the distance
Shouldn't the crater be great enough
          to bury the dead

Didn't we greet each other with our eyes
Don't our values begin with logic
Doesn't a clock cookie time

Up from the higher laws
Up until the chorus
Up in the sky it's a bird it's an eagle

Aren't we safer behind our keyboards
Aren't you sweet
Isn't this grand isn't this just like them

Don't you wish you knew what they were thinking
Don't you dare draw the gods

Wouldn't we be fools to fail to admire the screen
Wouldn't the fighting be bloodier without us
Were your coordinates correct

As long as your life lives
As long as you're asking
As if lightning struck down
As if distance could be clean

For now the fog lowers into the bay
For now the young engineers get tattoos
For now let them think it's brave

Now take one small step to your right
Now and that's an order
Now the winds hush
and you gust upon this earth

Fire Drill

I hope you have a month
to read the first fifteen chapters
of your own autobiography
they're about an atom.
Some say the sun
meant more then.

Today a few more trees are scheduled
to release their fall collections.
I don't have a swatch
for their nesting instinct.
I don't have the right crayon
for insomnia.

When I say you are this morning's incumbent
I mean accomplice.
When I swipe down with my thumb
to refresh the present
the Next Now arrives in the nick of time.

Next Now, heal us with opportunity.
Next Later, assure us our preferences have been saved.

What if I really am a suspension bridge
and by standing here
I make my most profound gesture
toward the world?
What if the sun were on a game show—
could anyone stop it?

I shouldn't talk this way.
Twinkle twinkle everyone outside.
You wanted a revolution,

you're getting an operating system update.
The past tense of *to be* is *was*.
You can check *was* off your bucket list.

To Be Transmitted by Fax

Like a movie that begins
in an isolated polar research facility,
R.J. MacReady asking the crew
tough questions about
the odd Malamute that's wandered in
off the tundra—when suddenly
the generator blows—
I like it when the lights go out.
I like shopping for groceries
with a storm on the way
making choices I'll question for days,
everyone's in a rush
and the coffee's about to run out.
I like imagining you
grocery shopping in the rain
in a mid-sized coastal town
where I don't know the names
of the regional chains
or the shortcut through the park
where the kids play a game
for hours before realizing
no one's keeping score.
In the corner drugstore
there's a yellowing machine
that appears to have heard
it all before, no urgent news
coming in over the transom.
But from the other side of the hills
there's the sound of chopper blades
and a flickering searchlight.
When you press
the machine's green button
you can hear the song
of a line left open.

Poem for an Antique Korean Fishing Bobber

Little glass planet,
I like picking you up.
As if I'm holding my own thought,
one blown molten with a puff
of some craftsman's breath—is it still inside you?
You are a beautiful bauble it's hard to imagine
anyone hurling you into the sea,
but eventually we all have a job to do.
I think of the early mornings and storm warnings
you braved to find the village dinner.
I don't remember carrying you
home on the plane from Seoul,
crew dozing behind the cockpit door,
autopilot engaged—what were they dreaming of?
I don't even know what shore
you washed up on: Busan, Incheon, Samcheok.
Are you glad we made you a home here so far
from the sea? is a question I won't ask in case
your answer is the one you don't want to give.
I love how perfectly you fit in my hand,
at first cold, and the way the morning looks
through you, as green and cloudy
as an unknown we no longer fear.
But I wouldn't want to be held up
to the sun either, not because I'm a monster,
but because I, too, am translucent and trusting,
and mistake both for the truth.
Beneath our lives there are sordid undulations
and embraces brief and sweet,
a nearly invisible line connecting us to the fleet,
with every breath worth saving,
like the sip of air inside us
full of an old sea's grace

or the ancient word hidden in our lungs
that once released back into the wild
will finally set us free.

What the Cold Wants

Complete mind control,
though it might begin Off-Broadway,
in a simple ceviche, or a mostly believable alibi.
Generally speaking, what the cold wants
is ridiculous. The problem with the cold
is that it comes from more of it.
It's divisible only by one and itself.
The cold is not invited
to many weddings.
Among the cold's lifetime
achievements: every touch
of a stethoscope, zero for twelve
from the beyond the arc, Shackleton's last note.
According to experts, the average
temperature of the known universe
is negative 454.76 degrees Fahrenheit.
Room temperature is a miracle.
That's what the cold wants you to believe,
that it's perfectly normal
and should be allowed to feel
right at home as it slithers under a door
to begin making a meal of your toes.
Like a hungry predator, the cold knows
to save the warm, wet heart for last.
The cold is a form of surveillance.
Its primary ingredient is time.
Safe at headquarters, the scientist
listens to the batteries in the radio collar
slowly die, but she knows
the wolf is out there still.
From you, the cold wants nothing
but in.

Roll Call

Present	Absent	
☐	☐	The gods sitting around reading *The Brand Called You*.
☐	☐	The gods watching us sleep and calling it "marathon training."
☐	☐	The gods chasing one another at the off-leash god park.
☐	☐	The gods looking into three-way mirrors so they can see their own butts.
☐	☐	The gods cursing us for pulling up dandelions.
☐	☐	The gods updating their secret maps of lost mittens.
☐	☐	The gods we mistakenly call sparrows.
☐	☐	The gods raising the prime interest rate another third.
☐	☐	The gods whispering: *Bleed out, and you blend right in.*
☐	☐	The gods amusing themselves by making the sound of your own name sound suddenly strange to you.
☐	☐	The gods who, after inventing the seahorse, largely quit.
☐	☐	The gods A/B testing new ways to monetize the obituaries.
☐	☐	The gods resting their defense on reasonable force.
☐	☐	The gods who can wave at a laser beam to dispense paper towels.
☐	☐	The gods in monogrammed bathrobes worried they've developed Resting God Face.
☐	☐	The gods brunching in America.
☐	☐	The gods, for now, among us.

Substitution

If only life weren't so confusing.
If I can't leave town with you,
here's an old record instead.
I can't miss anyone
who doesn't adore Slim Gaillard.
At first I was sure
I was going to grow up to be a pilot.
Today I don't know
who most of you people are—
and I thought I was God's chosen creature!
Like the piglet raised by a farm cat
whose mission in life
has become sunning on the porch
and acting aloof,
maybe inside every hog is a kitten.
As inside every wide receiver is a ballerina,
and inside every ballerina a swan
who is really a banished tzarina
tending to her colony of bees.
Any sauce comes with a swap out,
each lunch sack its secrets,
overdressed greens instead of fries,
another poem made out of ideas, not things.
A whistle blows and Coach nods
at the skinny kid on the end of the bench.
The figure skater does a double
instead of a triple and loses a tenth.
The hydrogen nuclei fuse
and now it's helium,
and when it fills the balloons
at the brat's birthday
his aunt's house doesn't seem
so horrible anymore.

My heart is a jackrabbit.
There is no trick: the way to eat fire
is you just eat fire.

I Can Do It All in My Lifetime

If I were to say the subjunctive is indistinguishable
from the machinations of morning itself,
would that put me even more under its spell?
In the repair-shop garage, the most broken-down cars
sleep on the top bunk, while on the edge of town,
pylons trim the highway to one lane, stopping traffic
for miles, all for a steamroller abandoned in the rain.
It's as close to forever as it's possible to know.
Have you ever felt so alone that it was oddly also
impossible to be only yourself? Then you know
what it's like to not have a name, only a sense of lightness
and a suspicion that everything is uncalled for,
and for reasons no one can understand we still believe
that for our children it will not be too late.

Ode to the Future

Of my people, it's true, I imagine you
among them, which is as close as I get
to believing in heaven, so I'm not so alone.
Fuck this government. Fuck honey mustard.
Fuck the new advanced whitening formula.
If this is what I know, does it make me
anything more than another dumb pilgrim
who hasn't lived through a single potato blight?
Lucky me, I rarely dream about the past,
nor have I reached the shore
of Great Conclusions, how long
will that last? I'm no more done with joy
than I am gravity, there are things
I'll never let them take, there's a photo
of my daughter locked inside a safe
behind a velvet painting
in the smoky backroom office of my skull.
It makes my head swell, as if everything is steamy,
or we're on a schooner
without any knowledge of knots.
There are no do-overs, every moment arrives
with the sheen of the new,
so let's make America a set of problems
we can admit exists again, and still have the will
to solve, we can get better at being alive,
you can learn a lot from being around horses,
you have to let the fury melt away
and stand in the sun.

Fickle Sun, Loyal Shadow

Another warm weekday waiting
for an alarm the firemen gossip

and wash their truck
a fresh breeze moves in

to shampoo our murmurs
language pays the world

lip service it's impossible to get
the same haircut twice

in the hallway mirror
the ceiling fan spins

in the opposite direction
cooling the next world

My bugle knows how
to play one song

and it's "Wake Up Motherfucker"
there's a lesson in that

you have to perform
what you already are

you've got to shake that moneymaker
the microwave flashes 4:52 4:52 4:52

a memorial to its life's great failure
I have one hypothesis

you have to be willing to start
with a guess

About heaven
I'm not so sure

can it really be more beautiful
than light or breakfast

in the morning the firefighters
fill a steel dish with water

from a filthy hose
to leave it on the walk

for the neighborhood dogs
no one takes a drink

if you look down into the dish
it holds the sky

If I lean back far enough
and close my eyes I vanish

no one taught me how
I was trying to describe the taste of water

without eternity there is no hour
and without the hour no moment

to watch the wind move through
these trees like Texas politics

I'm trying to imagine a reason
to defend both sides in the new war

these homes don't have cellars
the children are braver

Stepping outside feels
greedy like freckle season

is coming to an end
what have we been put on earth for

is not a dumb question it's an invitation
for dumb answers

the longer the limousine
the less wealthy the passengers

the rudest diners
choose Sunday for brunch

I love you so much
our toothbrushes are touching

The garage door rises
but the great red truck

has already gone I have
yet to sleep in a bed

able to contain me
a knife that lands

with its blade in the earth
will make no enemies

promises use the exact same words
as lies I can throw

two kinds of shadows in Texas
too short and long

Is there any way to wake
other than alarmed

each scent is the memory
of a previous experience

the perfumist is a ghostwriter
for the air

always smell the left arm first
it's closer to the heart

the fire department tried
to hire her she said no

unless you're fighting
flowers

Is there any way to wake
other than disappointed

to speak the same language
as weather leads curtains

through another dress rehearsal
a magician licks his fingertips

the safecracker sands his down
learn to look down into the water

to love to see the sky
and you won't fear loneliness

when the Forgetmenaut feels lonely
he looks up into his sky and sees us

There's an old mirror
abandoned in the alley

displaying more alley
but significantly less sky

where a stray cat hidden
beneath a parked car knows

the whole world
is a thunderstorm

we're ancient marine life
on the move we keep pulling

fish from the sea and still
the waters rise

The orange plyons
have been pulled from the street

the cell tower repair
allows the news to resume

its wicked speed down
at the playground the monkey

bars busy themselves dividing
sunlight into equal servings

the toothpaste manufacturer copyrights
Wintergreen and poetry shrugs

I won't take no for an answer
I asked you if this will last forever

It rains and the firefighters
sense an irrelevance

they can remember the days
when one of them drove

the truck and another drove
the rear of the truck

each trained to turn the wheel
away from his colleague

is steering something the rain is
so too the sky and not having plans

with everything falling into place
solitude is something or is it fire

Few clues no real way
of knowing no news

from the Forgetmenaut
nothing in the mailbox

or reason to check twice
no sleeves to pull

our hands back into
during a gentle morning argument

no one able to lift their gaze
from their phone

that bird looks weird
the other bird sounds weird

Outside the fire station
the morning explodes into laundry

drying from a rusty chin-up bar
the Forgetmenaut wishes

he could see you too
air conditioner drips keep time

cell phones ping
with urgent insignificances

at the market a pickup truck drops
its ordinance of watermelons

next to a broken-down car
playing the role of Someday

I walked past the post office
on my way to walking

past the fire station
I can't remember what it was

I urgently sent
myself into this world to do

the great red truck
is parked outside

on the driveway for a wash
they named it Engine No. 9

across both doors
we will never forget

This evening shows signs
of early onset darkness

we see ourselves
as others see us

in our laundry
the Forgetmenaut draws

an architecture of the infinite
inside her dresser a piano teacher

keeps a tiny glass bottle
and inside that glass bottle

are all of her daughter's
baby teeth

Sunlight swallows succulents
the birds trapped in the airport

can't fly on planes
I'll be having the usual

as if it were ever my choice
I'm seceding from *was*

in order to form a more
perfect union with *is*

or could it be with *will be*
the blanket folded at the foot

of the bed is an understudy
for imminent change

I've decided I will king this block
they will greet us with sweets and flowers

the scene is best performed in the dark
the suitcase is empty beneath the bed

the Forgetmenaut reports
it all looks so fragile from space

I've lost sight of you shadow
saint of myself

the next indefinite article will play
the role of Object Approaching

a white bike chained to a red stop sign
we're fools to think we can tame our ghosts

The fire station was constructed
when people and their things

were smaller though not fire
it's still night and it has become

a still night the quiet sky
appears to hold one star

that's technically a planet
it's everything the Forgetmenaut

promised to us when the great
red truck backs into the garage

the ladder scrapes against the jamb
and makes a spark

Last night the firefighters forgot
to bring in the silver dish

from the sidewalk
it has become a bath

for birds while bees in the amaranth
do their morning work

there have been signs all along
Rich Fernandez for Mayor

Kathie Tovo for City Council
Piano Lessons for Beginners

the sign warning of an approaching sign
reads STOP AHEAD

I'm one-thousand-and-one birds
a figment of your imagination

a shadow that glides over the street
the sun that pushes it along

into the next moment
where time discovers

a bit more self-confidence
and firefighters mow the station lawn

riding tiny red mowers
as if in practice

right thought write words right poem
innocence is not a victimless crime

This is yours and yours to keep
for as long as you care to remember

the Forgetmenaut can't wipe
that look off his face it takes a lifetime

to remember being a person
is two-thirds being a pattern

the phone poles here T T T T
no longer carry conversation

though there's still more to say
I want you to know I walked here

walked at one point through
a face full of bees

They've taken the trash
as far as the curb taken the pledge

as far as the flag I've taken
your advice and called mom

time will have its way
what we can't see will save us

sometimes you have to walk
with a rock in your shoe to learn

they ran out of presidents to name
the streets after so now people

come and go among signs for trees
beginning with Ash

Goodnight moon goodnight Ash
goodnight great red truck

goodnight late capitalism goodnight Dallas
over Houston by seven in the third

goodnight CEOs giving
one another another raise

goodnight Forgetmenaut
making a last orbit of the house

sounds lost in the air
each tree dreaming

of outer space lowering itself to us
you try to name this or I will

When our great fire finally arrives
it will make no sound

I went outside to see if outside
was still around and it was

a lemon tree dressed in December ice
like a girl in her grandmother's jewelry

you can say forget-me-not until it's empty
but there's only so much to extinguish

while remaining present enough
to see the job through

a child arrives for a lesson the teacher
knows the piano does all the teaching

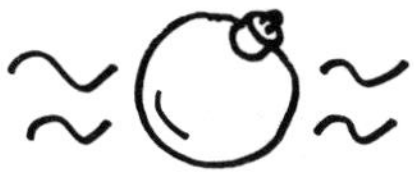

Inside the Compulsion to Wonder Lurks the Will to Survive

Once awake, I tend to like it.
A puddle can recognize me. Then I look up
and I'm as anonymous as the sky.
And yet, in my hands, this terrible orb glows.
The ships, it reports, can now sail
straight through the Arctic, filthy bears
clinging to shriveling rafts of ice.

Tell me the truth, what does anyone care
inside the barber shop this morning
where everyone wants the regular again,
combs swimming in little blue aquariums.
What if this isn't late capitalism, but early?

One idea is to set the clocks ahead
one hour so we're closer to knowing
how it turns out. Another is the Roman ides,
or the 72 *kō* of Japan. *Mist starts to linger.*
Great rains sometimes fall.
The Buddhists have a word for it,
but the moment it's defined,
the thing itself vanishes.

The more we ask of this world
rises up through us, like an evaporation.
When I asked you what day it was,
you said the day after yesterday.
No matter where we move the glass vase,
it leaves a ring.

Everything I've Learned So Far

Isn't it so Norway
the way the snow falls
slowly on the freeway,
low lights traffic hum
inching along
with the inevitability
of an aging democracy.
Like a fury surrendering to
a stillness we've never known,
like our favorite movie,
or the invention of braille,
abstract expressionism,
and the full-court press.
It all belongs to us now:
panthers sad
we call them tigers,
moms sad
we don't call them much at all.
All house flies buzz in the key of F.
It's unknown how long
a lobster can live.
Puppies stop being cute at two.
I have no problem wearing lipstick
so long as I can apply it
using your mouth.
You can close your eyes
and place a sugar cube
on your tongue
and swear you've tasted a star.
Whatever happens next,
wave your little wand,
claim magic.

Selected Poems

Poem with Its Fist Raised

Poem Composed of Ash and Bone

Poem Etched in Marble

    —in Repose

    —with Plum Blossoms and Birds

    —with a Sword in Its Mouth

Poem in a Summer Kimono

Poem, Silver Comb and Pin

Study for a Poem

Poem with a Partially Obstructed View of the Academy

    [Not on View]

    [On Loan]

    [Removed for Cleaning]

Poem ("I'll Read Two More")

Poem of St. Paul with a Book and a Candle Facing Away from the Door

Poem in Black Ink, Brush and Gray Wash on Paper, Incised for Transfer
    onto Linen, and Presented on a Panel

Poem Partially Composed over an Older Poem

    Poem (Fragment)

    Poem (Shard)

Poem (Relic)

Poem (Paperweight)

Poem (Apology)

Poem Whispered While Being Blown into Molten Glass, Then Shattered

    —in Black Gloves and Edwardian Evening Ensemble

    —with a Porcelain Cover

    —with Eight Views from *The Tale of Genji*

Poem [Unclaimed, Undated, and Unfinished]

Poem Approaching the End

Poem with the Words Left Out

    —with the Words Put Back In

Poem Attributed to a 16th Century Flemish Poet

Poem [Gift of Mr. and Mrs. Harold M. Cartwright]

Poem That Sounds Suspiciously Familiar

Poem Seen from Behind

Poem in Profile, Adorned with Silk Scarving, Looking Thoughtfully into the Distance, Chin Resting on Fist

Why I Don't Have Any Tattoos

I'm still here trying to get it right.
Now that there's enough slow
evening snow to allow
a streetlamp to steal a scene,
but like its glow, even that thought
only goes so far.
The tired Chinese restaurants
on Lake Street closed at nine,
which is so Midwestern of them.
It may be too late for history but not luck,
a scratch-off ticket from SuperAmerica
where SuperMom's coffee
is 49 cents with gas, snow
hitting my face
like the needles touching down
on the skin of the invincible
inside Leviticus Tattoos.
Already I'm a blue butterfly
landing on your shoulder blade,
I'm a bald eagle carrying lightning bolts
across my chest. At some point
I'm going to rise up
into these trees and turn gold.
What I thought I needed
seems so far away and harmless,
there isn't anything
I'd throw away or give back,
and the nights are getting shorter now,
which is a start.

The Impossibility of Sending You a Postcard from Mumbai

It's the swirling way this red boat circles
its mooring and gently knocks,
leaving no mark on the world.
As dependably as these letters appear

then begin to vanish like the decoded glyphs
of ancient Hindi tablets, chiseled from cliffs
and translated into tiny packets, passed hand to hand like contraband
through a century of sometimes sleepless nights.

To say something is different is to create fate.
If right now proves anything
about back then, it's destiny,
and I'm on the other side of the world

full of sun and a thousand things I can't bring you.
As if anyone could describe a single wave.
In curling toward shore, this one reveals itself, kneels,
then scatters in confusion, but even that's not quite right.

Still it would have been a shame not to notice this
and try to map it for you, and now
it's another thing to leave behind between us.
An ocean, mostly blue.

Litany

When she asked me where fairies live, I said trees.

The president nods off on his golden loo.

The senator from South Carolina won't shut up.

Here's another virgin with a list of baby names picked out.

Here's another corporate lobbyist rewriting the tax code.

Maybe if I hum a few bars?

Brittany.

Brayden.

Aiden.

Litany.

They ring the market's opening bell by hand.

They sell the bundled debt fiber-optically.

For the rest of your life, every cashier will ask if you want to round up.

They're rebranding butter as I Can't Believe It's Not I Can't Believe It's Not Butter.

They're rebranding death as Nature's No. 1 Clinically Proven Anti-Aging Formula.

Arms wide: *Shavasana*.

In the moment the airbag deploys, the car sends the satellite a signal.

As the ambulance receives the coordinates, its radio crackles.

Bed in Winter

First thought, dark thought.
Now night, an old tune,
so soon a truer sleep returns,
one intent on placating its own cravings.
We dream the moon into being.
Great ships ghost the horizon,
then vanish at lights-out.

Among the trees, spiders
hang tiny ladders spun from silver:
a new shift of creatures is taking over.
There's a clearing overhead
as we prepare to assume a place in the sky.
No one speaks. There's too much to be said.
We're never more than nearly awake.
We're evolving neither from nor toward
this nothingness—our eternity has simply arrived,
but will any of us remember it later?
As the sun fights back, our children grow
weary of their own thoughts,
and rubbing their eyes, push stuffed dogs
away with their feet.

Ziggurat

Because it was the most beautiful thing,
I built my fortress from snow.
It's my most complete thought. It won't last long.

Against the white you can't miss
the shelves of books, nor the guests' stunned looks
as I chip their breath off the ceilings.

Turns out I'm my own best servant.
In the kitchen I cut crusts from sandwiches,
a forgotten permission slip in my pocket.

When I shout "dinner's ready," the rooms go silent.
There's no drawbridge, no trebuchet into outer space.
Eventually everyone makes a flying leap.

In one story of Osiris, to become an immortal,
you simply act like one. It was written on the walls
of the pyramids, and some of them still stand.

At night, home is indistinguishable from night,
but when I shine my headlights right at it,
it looks like diamonds.

Now Where Were We?

In this weather it's tough
to make a clean getaway
in stolen bishop's slippers,
the bridesmaids smashing wine glasses,
trucks not thinking twice
about driving onto the ice
and making a bonfire
out of used Christmas trees.
Scoreboard: noon sun, moon none.
Hoods up and hats on,
fresh track marks in the talk track,
lost walkie-talkies talking in tongues,
come in come in, got your ears on?
Even though we're mostly eyes.
Even though we shouldn't be trusted with teeth.
Somewhere far from here there's a beach
where cormorants chase the shags
and beauty has tricked itself into believing
it's immune from extinction
in a way that ends each day
in a sunset that doesn't make you feel
as if you aren't keeping up,
someone grandfathered you in.
Try as we may, it's clear
we're going to experience everything
not quite twice.

Fall In

This is my love letter to the world,
someone call us a sitter.
We're going to be here awhile.
We're going to have traffic
coming up on the eights,
the latest news at the top of the hour,
and this early in the night
when the bats circle the steeple,
they look as pale
as my more unvarnished thoughts,
that one about what
to do with bacon grease,
or how best to approach
Neoplatonism in the dark.
If you're looking for them,
the cowboys left for the noodle bar,
the ballerinas are down
on the ground level,
circling the baggage carousel.
I'm not going to turn this upside-down
so you can see
the answers in the margin.
Time is working against us,
but it makes us love it more.
Everything I've ever touched,
even seaweed.
Whatever I've thrown away
and then desperately wanted back:
old boots, cinnamon-baked pears,
bumper cars at midnight, Berlitz,
Becky Razzidlo's basement
before her parents got home.
The first time I walked
out onto a lake in the middle of January
I knew I could go anywhere.

April Light

The movers have arrived, terrified of books.
Maybe spooked by the bird feeder on its side,
spilled champagne coupe of a sodden god
abandoned at the curb with a mattress,
as if someone outgrew sleep. The last snow
retreats into the earth to wait us out, or does it?
We can't be sure. Swim lesson registration is full.
Raise the window sash enough to allow in
the present tense: where are the cowards now?
In the park, they pull the tarp off the carousel.
Our dreams don't change much.
A purple elephant chases a pink seahorse in circles.
Four white stallions pull an empty chariot
to a spot where the youngest know to wait.

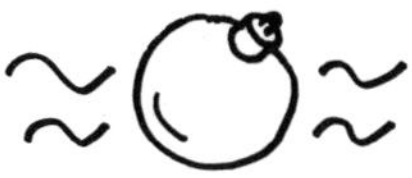

Trace

1.

More or less alone
now wishing for time

to sing itself into a strain
of thought stored in trace

amounts growing gradually
into gestures inking the book

that holds the pages
with thin blue lines.

Are you with me so far?
Good, it's almost over.

To serve you better, our terms
and conditions have changed,

or so poetry's technology
is always announcing,

its chipped crystals poised
to detonate and melt back into

the unsaid after releasing light
from a sense of the collective.

So Sundays being what they are
(a prologue that Saturday

surrenders to) this desert night
making its final appeal,

it's as if that's all there is,
a bit winter but not quite spring,

everywhere between us the sound
of no ground being given

on heavy trading
as the markets stumble

under indifferent skies.
There's nothing I fear more

than my own intentions.
I don't have much advice for you here.

On your first trip to Europe,
see the great churches.

On your second, mostly drink wine.
When a mother is grieving,

the oldest daughter
should enter the room first.

A scorpion is never
just resting there. Some of you

will be disappointed to learn
I didn't write this

to "express my feelings,"
though I hope you will be

the same people relieved
to discover it doesn't require

a skeleton key.
It's a little space

opening up in language,
full of permission.

2.

I don't believe in
the paranormal any more

than I do the idea that a poem
can mend the world,

but I also refuse every offer
of surrender presented to me

by my own disbeliefs.
I've been reading

of the icebergs dispatched
with urgent news

drowning before reaching us,
and of our prehistoric ancestors

sleeping in trees
with the bowerbirds

that know how to navigate
by stars. Like Saturn,

which I yesterday saw glow
through the McDonald

Observatory telescope, its rings
that I assumed were asteroid belts

turn out to be mostly dust
and great mists of ice,

two of the rings spinning defiantly
in opposition to the collective.

I've been following
the latest quantum experiments

that isolated two diamonds
and bombarded one with electrons,

still altering the other,
proving "spooky action

at a distance" is real.
Describing this

to my wife over the phone
I could hear our daughter

clearing the dinner plates
and it made me wonder

what should have been said differently.
Inside my pockets is a small cloth

I use to wipe dust from my glasses
and enough space

to hide my harmless, cold fists.
Outside this house

I can see tumbleweeds
rolling down the street

and since I walked among them
probably also tumbleweed dust

somewhere in my chest.
We're trapped inside diamonds

but when we think of one another
we can make the diamonds spin.

3.

If we belong to anything in the universe
it's to our own music,

which isn't a place or thing,
but a disruption to the norm,

loose patterns of displacement
and recovery

creating regions of high and then
low pressure, a plot

that writes itself, like weather.
I can still hear the dishes

being put away in St. Paul,
stacked like hats into old cabinets.

The sun is burning off the clouds
pressing in from Chihuahua.

Last night, when I tried
and failed to see

the Marfa Lights, I succeeded
in preserving their mystery.

From the corners of my eyes
the glow of fellow phones,

an eerie phenomena I find
difficult to explain,

even as I, too, used a screen
to trace a brighter path

through the desert dark
back to my car.

I tried to describe this
to my mother over the phone

but mostly listened to serrated
packets of digital information

scramble in a satellite signal
that remained clear enough

to broadcast the sound
of her curious cough.

Can you imagine a total absence
of mystery light so distinct

as to create a truer darkness?
This shared thought,

if understood as a virtual
sound, can abbreviate

the space between us,
creating a form of weather.

4.

I already wish
this were beginning.

Any omissions here aren't born
from a lack of watching

the mountains in the dark
and hoping for a sign.

What part of understand
don't you remember?

Swipe down from the top
to view your notifications.

In an ocean to the south,
a great dish pointed

toward a globular star cluster
beams out our cosmic message.

Hello, hello, is anyone out there?
The night sky returns

a dial tone of dendritic light
and lacunae.

My mother's cough is more strange
the clearer the images become

beamed back from space
inside her chest.

Hello, hello, odd cough,
what have you visited my mother for?

The scientists analyze the signal
and so far agree: all static.

A Texas wind pushes
old branches against

the steel roof to scrawl
their illegible prescriptions.

The more I wonder,
the less I seem to know,

but this is my temple,
and I keep my temple clean.

5.

If there really is another world,
maybe we can walk to the edge

of town where beyond
the FOR SALE sign

marking the last empty lot
is a rusty barbed-wire fence

the desert wind can pass
through without a scratch.

At midnight, a hundred televisions
woosh back into darkness.

No aircraft floating out there,
no cell-phone-tower beacons

pulsing with favorites.
So you can get a good look

at the aberrant spray of stars
and the space slowly swallowing them.

Can it be true
our primary job

here on earth is to wait?
If there really is another world,

maybe all the languages are there too,
still desperate to perform,

sentences full of bright shards,
straining to shorten distances

by opening up staticky channels.
It's odd we assume whatever is out there

will be able to understand us
any better than we do.

From the mountains there's a little glow,
like a campfire, or maybe old headlights.

6.

Before I left for Texas
I watched my daughter dance

her last ballet of the season,
yellowed spotlights

tracing the movements of children
dressed as antique soldiers,

ground troops deployed
to clear and hold space

for the sugar plum fairies to spin
as the boy suspended high above

sprinkled phony snow
onto a real stage,

and it became quiet enough to hear
the oldest man cough,

as if already wondering
whether it was time to show

his grandchildren the yellowest
part of his teeth and ask them

when and how in this world
they would begin making money.

I don't believe in the paranormal,
but I do believe in poems,

another system of haunts,
pulling the rip cord

inside your head
so the aperture opens

to allow in more light.
There is a way to practice patience

so that it verges on disobedience,
your last thought creating the next,

any association codifying the theory.
This was always

going to be about possibilities,
one definition of love.

We made this together, this we,
more or less alone now

slowly beginning to spin.
Like in a museum

when the visitors whisper
without being told

out of respect for what
lives there larger and lingers

at night long after
the guards hang up

their navy blazers,
dust circling in the moonlight

falling through the courtyard's
glass ceiling for no one to see,

something big enough
to ignore us right back,

maybe drifting oceanward,
where it returns to an inkling.

Acknowledgments

Thank you to the editors of the following publications for providing homes to earlier versions of these poems, some under different titles:

The Academy of American Poets Poem-a-Day	*"L'Avenir Est Quelque Chose"*
Bat City Review	"Everything I've Learned So Far" "Fall In"
Boog City Reader	"Roll Call"
Columbia Poetry Review	"Idaho"
Conduit	"Selected Poems" "Litany"
Denver Quarterly	"Substitution"
Forklift, Ohio	"Ode to the Future"
The Freshwater Review	"The Impossibility of Sending You a Postcard from Mumbai"
Horsethief	"Fire Drill"
The Iowa Review	"What the Cold Wants"
jubilat	"Poem for an Antique Korean Fishing Bobber"
Poetry East	"Bed in Winter"
Poetry Northwest	"Now Where Were We?" "April Light"
St. Ann's Review	"Why I Don't Have Any Tattoos"

"Fickle Sun, Loyal Shadow" first appeared as a chapbook published by Sixth Finch. Thank you to editors Rob MacDonald and Dara Cerv.

"To Be Transmitted by Fax" first appeared in *If You've Received This Message in Error: Dispatches from the North American Fax Registry, Volume 1*, the creation of artist Andy Sturdevant, and the last known fax-delivery-only art publication in the US (www.facsimilepress.org).

"Ziggurat" first appeared on the cassette-only psychodrone album *Predawn to Postdusk* by Umbral. Thank you to Daniel Hales and Spork Press.

"Bed in Winter" is after Robert Louis Stevenson's "Bed in Summer."

More thank yous: To the Lannan Foundation for a Residency Fellowship in Marfa, Texas, that aided in the completion of this book. To the Minnesota State Arts Board for an Artist Initiative Grant that provided time and space to write. To my colleagues at the University of Texas at Austin for their generosity while I served as visiting associate professor in 2014.

To my editor Jeff Shotts and everyone at Graywolf Press for their support. To Amanda Nadelberg, Ed Bok Lee, sam sax, and Dean Young for their careful attention to these poems. To Yuji Agematsu, whose marvelous art is featured on the book's cover.

To Kathy and Scarlett Moon most of all.